LANDMARKS IN HISTORY

THE TOWER OF LONDON

A 2000-YEAR HISTORY

IVAN LAPPER

GEOFFREY PARNELL

ROYAL
ARMOURIES

OSPREY
PUBLISHING

Contents

- AD 40 - Before the Romans — 4

- AD 200 - The Roman City Fortified — 7

- AD 400 - Twilight of the Roman City — 10

- AD 886 - Alfred and the Danish Threat — 13

- AD 1080 - The Conqueror's Castle — 16

- AD 1200 - The Tower Enlarged — 19

- AD 1240 - The Classic Castle — 22

- AD 1300 - Apogee of the Medieval Castle — 25

- AD 1547 - The Tudor Power House — 28

- AD 1700 - Showplace of the Nation — 31

- AD 1841 - The Great Conflagration — 34

- AD 1890 - Remedievalisation of the Castle — 37

- AD 1940 - The Castle at War — 40

- AD 2000 - The Tower Today — 43

Tower Plan — 46

Introduction

IVAN LAPPER ARCA has established himself as a leading illustrator in the field of historical reconstruction. His work, particularly his architectural and landscape impressions, may be seen in museums, historic buildings and ancient monuments across Britain. Ivan Lapper uses archaeological and documentary evidence to make cardboard models, from which the final artwork is created.

DR GEOFFREY PARNELL is Keeper of Tower History at the Royal Armouries, Tower of London, and a former English Heritage Inspector of Ancient Monuments. He has undertaken various excavations at the Tower and has written extensively on the archaeology of the site and the history of its buildings and institutions.

The Tower of London occupies a special place in the history of the English nation and through this association has become one of the most famous and visited buildings in the world. Popular images of ravens, Yeoman Warders, Crown Jewels and the myth of a grim fortress-prison do not, however, do justice to the castle's complex story, including its long and fascinating building history. The history of the Tower begins in 1066, but the form of the first Norman castle was to a large extent determined by buildings erected and modified by the Romans hundreds of years earlier.

During the past 40 years our understanding of the history of the Tower and its site has been transformed. The great increase in the study of buried remains and standing structures, together with advances in dating techniques such as tree-ring analysis, has produced a wealth of new information. The Tower is one of the best-documented buildings in the country, and the study of surviving written and drawn records has yielded much additional information. New research continues to shed more light on the past and in the process challenges established views and interpretations.

To celebrate the start of the new millennium the Royal Armouries has commissioned the artist Ivan Lapper to produce fourteen impressions of the Tower of London and its site at different times over the last 2000 years. These views, incorporating the results of recent research, provide a dramatic representation of the development of one of England's most important historical sites from the close of the prehistoric period to the present.

Acknowledgements

The authors would like to thank Dr Edward Impey for information and ideas concerning architecture detail and Mrs Bridget Clifford for help and assistance with the draft text and picture research.

- AD 40 -
Before the Romans

Cunobelinus AD10–42 'Britannorum Rex' from a bronze coin

A prehistoric body gives clues about the earliest human settlement on the site of the future Tower of London

During the prehistoric period the southern margins of the site of the future Tower of London formed a marshy area on the north bank of the river Thames. Archaeological excavations in the south-east corner of the Inmost Ward, close to the Lanthorn Tower, in 1955 and 1976 revealed a noticeable bend in the line of the river bank beneath accumulated layers of sand and gravel. From the tops of these deposits pieces of worn pottery and flint flakes were recovered – the earliest evidence we have for human activity in the area.

Towards the end of the prehistoric period the river retreated to the south leaving the area dry. The discovery of a large pit, yielding flint flakes and Iron Age pottery, and a shallow grave containing the skeleton of a young male, 13–16 years of age, demonstrated that there was human occupation in the vicinity. The body was arranged in a semi-flexed position with legs partly drawn up and pushed to one side and a ring was found among

The prehistoric bank of the river Thames revealed during excavations in the Inmost Ward in 1976. The brick-lined pit in the top right-hand corner dates from the late 17th or early 18th century. (G. Parnell)

the finger bones. Radiocarbon analysis of the bone indicates that it dates back to no earlier than the beginning of the 1st century AD. This, together with the style of the burial and the sequence of deposits that sealed the grave, suggests that the youth died just before the Roman invasion of AD 43.

Prior to the Roman invasion the lands on the north side of the Thames were shared between the Trinovantes and the Catuvellauni, and it is probably to one of these Belgic tribes that the young man buried on the Thames foreshore belonged. It is unlikely that he (or the people who buried him) came from far afield, or that he was associated with any major settlement. Instead, as the illustration here suggests, home was probably an isolated farmstead on the gentle slope of hill leading down to the Thames and his final resting-place.

A late Iron Age burial discovered north-west of the Lanthorn Tower during excavations in 1976. (G. Parnell)

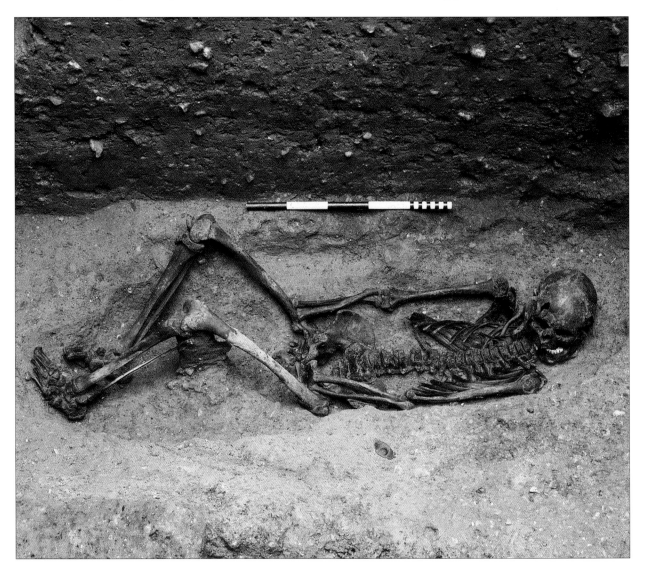

The Roman City Fortified

Septimus Severus 193–211 Emperor, from a silver denarius

The thriving Roman city of Londinium spreads across the site, and is surrounded by a great defensive wall

The area now occupied by the Tower was not immediately affected by the Roman invasion of AD 43 and the foundation of London (*Londinium*). The earliest developments lay just beyond the tidal reach of the Thames and round the river Walbrook some 800m (875 yards) to the west. The early settlement became a trading port which, according to the celebrated historian Tacitus, was 'packed with traders'.

In AD 60 the new town met a disastrous end at the hands of the vengeful Boudicca and her Iceni followers. After several years of slow recovery *Londinium* began to expand rapidly and by the end of the first century it had become a thriving city with a great bridge over the Thames (near the present London Bridge), a forum (market-place), a vast basilica (town hall), an amphitheatre, public baths and a walled fort. The growth of the city eastwards also saw the marshy area of the Inmost Ward reclaimed by the end of the century – an act probably associated with the construction of some form of wharf under what is now the Outer Ward of the castle. This expansion may also have been linked to the construction of a substantial masonry building on ground now partly occupied by the White Tower. The excavated remains of this building occupy a position along the projected line of Great Tower St, a road of Roman origin that led to the centre of the City from somewhere out in the countryside to the east.

During the 2nd century a timber-framed house with painted plaster walls was constructed on the reclaimed land adjoining the riverfront. Some time after the middle of the century it was destroyed by fire and immediately replaced by another property of similar form and appearance. Around AD 200 the replacement building was deliberately demolished to help make way for one of Roman London's most enduring monuments – the City wall. This impressive structure, just over 2 miles (3km) in length, was constructed to protect the landward side of the city, perhaps at the instigation of Clodius Albinus, the governor of Britain who made an unsuccessful bid to become emperor, following the assassination of Commodus in AD 192.

Sections of the wall, which was strengthened by a V-shaped ditch to the outside and an earth bank to the inside, have been recorded at different times within the confines of the Tower. It is clear that the construction of the wall proceeded from north to south, i.e., towards the river, and that it terminated on or close to the site of the present Lanthorn Tower. Perhaps the most surprising aspect of the construction of this section of the wall is the fact that much of the masonry building near the south-east corner of the White Tower was allowed to remain standing. This highly unusual act may suggest that the building, or its owner, were of some importance.

A 2nd-century Roman intaglio, or gemstone, found during excavations in the Inmost Ward in 1976. Made of red jasper (17mm x 13mm x 2mm), the device is the goddess Athena (i.e., Roman Minerva) with Nike (Victoria) standing on her extended arm and a rearing serpent below. (G. Parnell)

- AD 400 -

Twilight of the Roman City

Flavius Honorius 395–423 Emperor of the West, from a gold solidus

The threat of Saxon sea-borne raids sees a strengthening of the Tower's riverside defences

During the second half of the 3rd century the defences of *Londinium* were strengthened by the addition of a defensive river wall. A section of the wall examined close to the Lanthorn Tower in 1977 was found to rest on a great number of oak piles. The growth rings of these piles were cross-matched with timbers recovered from beneath other parts of the river wall and dated to AD 255–70. Historically this was a period of grave trouble, for Britain formed part of the breakaway Gallic Empire that separated from Rome for fourteen years following the usurpation of Cassianus Postumus in AD 259. It was during this period that the threat of Saxon sea-borne raids first became acute, and a number of powerful forts are believed to have been constructed along the coast of southern England in the 270s and 80s in response to the growing menace.

During the last years of the 4th century a remarkable remodelling of the riverside defences close to the Lanthorn Tower was undertaken. A massive wall some 3.20m (10ft 6in) wide was erected 4m (13ft) to the north of the existing one,

which it presumably replaced. Some 14.50m (47ft) west of the landward wall it turned abruptly south at an angle of 105° to connect with the earlier wall. The effect was to create a promontory at the extreme angle of the defences guarding the river approach to the city. Perhaps intended to accommodate catapults, the promontory seems to have incorporated a small gate or postern in its west flank that provided access down onto the foreshore.

During excavations in 1976–77 and 1979 numerous late 4th-century coins were found in deposits beneath and against the wall, which securely date its construction to a period after AD 388–92. As such the wall not only represents the latest Roman defence so far identified in London, but the latest Roman military work yet found in Britain.

The remodelling of the river wall may be connected with the work of Stilicho, the Vandal general, who made a final effort to restore imperial order in Britain between AD 386 and 399. This is reflected in an edict issued by the Emperor Honorius in AD 396 authorising local authorities to rebuild and repair their fortifications using, if necessary, materials drawn from disused temples and other buildings. In this respect, rebuilt or repaired sections of the wall at the Tower and elsewhere along the city riverfront seem to have made generous use of second-hand stone taken from public buildings and other monuments. The same practice has been observed in the construction of bastions that were added to the eastern side of the landward wall – all perhaps part of a final effort to modernise and improve the defences of *Londinium* in the years leading up to the official Roman withdrawal from Britain.

The late 4th-century Roman riverside wall viewed from the east during excavations in 1977. (G. Parnell)

- AD 886 -

Alfred and the Danish Threat

Alfred the Great 871–99 from a coin c.886

After abandonment and decay in the 5th century, Alfred the Great orders the restoration of the city of London

In the first years of the 5th century Britain was in a perilous political and economic state. Most of the remaining Roman garrison departed for the Continent in AD 407, thereby allowing a barbarian onslaught to take place. Nobles and local councils were left to urge inhabitants to take up arms and defend themselves. In AD 410 these bodies appealed to the emperor Honorius for help, but with the Goths at the gates of Rome itself there was little Honorius could do except send his famous letter renouncing responsibility for the defence of Britain.

What the situation was in London at this time is not clear. Excavations behind the restored river wall at the Tower have revealed tantalising evidence for building work still continuing, while an official stamped silver ingot and gold coins of Honorius and Arcadius found nearby in 1777 may confirm the presence of a London Treasury mentioned in a late Roman document. It has been suggested that the south-east corner of the city, where the Tower now stands,

Wartime bombing disclosed this Saxon arch, perhaps dating from the 9th or 10th century, in the south-west corner of the church of All Hallows Barking on Tower Hill. (Museum of London Archaeological Service)

was transformed into a citadel of last retreat. Such developments are recorded in other Roman centres on the Continent, but until more is known the situation in London remains uncertain.

According to the Anglo-Saxon Chronicle the Britons of Kent fled to London after their defeat at the hands of the Saxons in 457. If they did, they would have found little comfort, for all the evidence suggests a city decayed and largely abandoned. The excavation of a late Roman house to the west of the Tower at Billingsgate provides an evocative picture. The building was abandoned in the first quarter of the 5th century and thereafter debris accumulated over the floors before decay caused the tiled roof to collapse. Subsequently the house received visitors, evidently scavengers, including a woman who lost a bronze brooch of a distinctive early Saxon form. Nearby, the riverfront lay abandoned, the wharves being slowly concealed by silts washed down from the hillside.

The establishment of St Paul's Cathedral in 604 was perhaps one of the first steps along the road to London's revival, but for the next 250 years the main Saxon settlement, *Lundenwic*, was situated along the Strand (*Akemannstraete*) to the west of the city. *Lundenwic*, which Bede referred to as 'a market of many people coming by land and sea', continued to grow until the middle of the 9th century when Viking raids encouraged its inhabitants to relocate within the walls of the old Roman city for protection.

In 871–72 the Danes occupied London, but in 886 the king of the West Saxons, Alfred the Great, expelled them and ordered the city to be restored. The strategic south-east corner, guarding the river approach, must have been a priority and the foundation of two known Saxon churches in the area, All Hallows Barking on Tower Hill and St Peter ad Vincula in the Tower itself, may date from this period.

- AD 1080 -

The Conqueror's Castle

William I 1066–82 from a silver penny minted in Hereford

The White Tower viewed from the south-east with the ruins of the Wardrobe Tower in the foreground. (Royal Armouries)

Work begins on the first Norman castle of the Conquest. The life of the mighty White Tower begins

After the riots that accompanied William the Conqueror's triumphant coronation in Westminster Abbey on Christmas Day 1066, his contemporary biographer, William of Poitiers, states that the king withdrew to Barking in Essex 'while certain fortifications were made against the fickleness of the vast and fierce population'. One of the three strongholds that the Norman invaders established in the City during the winter of 1066/7 was the future Tower of London, set within the south-east angle of the old Roman defences.

Excavations have revealed an early Norman ditch that would have been reinforced with an earthen rampart and wooden stockade and which indicates that the first castle enclosed an area of only 1¼ acres. It should be noted that when part of the Norman ditch was investigated in 1963–64 under the Parade Ground, behind the White Tower, it was found to truncate an earlier ditch. That feature, which probably enclosed a site on the ridge of the hill, has led to suggestions that some sort of Saxon fortification already existed in the area at the time of the Norman invasion.

If there was a pre-existing fortification in this corner of the City, the Norman engineers took no account of it, preferring instead to direct their line of defence to points along the Roman walls where bastions existed. Their enclosure must have contained the usual collection of lodgings, storehouses, stables, etc., although later rebuilding works have erased all trace of them. Indeed, apart from the ditch, the only evidence for the original castle may be some masonry repairs to the Roman river wall that have been recorded close to the Lanthorn Tower.

Most castles built during the Conquest included a 'motte' or artificial mound, but the Tower, its form partly determined by the Roman walls to the east and south, seems not to have had one. The main entrance was to the west, close to the south-west corner of the later White Tower and along the projected line of Great Tower St. Given its small size, there might have been an outer bailey, but again physical confirmation has yet to be found.

The history of the Tower of London as we know it today begins with the construction of the White Tower, the enormous structure that gave the castle its name. Work must have begun in, or shortly after, 1077 when it is recorded that Gundulf, Bishop of Rochester, was 'by command of King William the Great ... supervising the work of the great tower of London'. Architecturally the White Tower derives from the great towers, or *donjons*, that the rulers of Normandy had been creating for over 100 years to meet their residential, ceremonial and military needs. The White Tower was probably only half built by 1087 when its owner, and the greatest Norman ruler of all time, William the Conqueror, died following a riding accident.

Lower part of the original 11th-century Norman ditch discovered during excavations to the north of the Wakefield Tower in 1975. (G. Parnell)

- AD 1200 -

The Tower Enlarged

John 1199–1216 from a silver penny minted in Dublin

Chancellor Longchamp begins to enlarge the castle, but work is interrupted when the Tower is captured

An artist's impression of the forebuilding erected to protect the entrance to the White Tower in the 12th century. (Royal Armouries)

The Anglo-Saxon Chronicle mentions that in 1097 a wall was built about the Tower of London – presumably to replace the earth and timber rampart of the Conqueror's time. Otherwise little attention appears to have been paid to the castle by the second Norman ruler of England, William Rufus (1087–1100). In fact, recent investigations have shown that it was not until the following reign of Henry I (1100–35) that work on the White Tower itself was completed.

Henry II (1154–89), one of England's greatest castle builders, appears to have been responsible for certain repairs to the fabric of the castle, including some of the royal lodgings that had been erected in the bailey to the south of the White Tower. Henry may also have been responsible for the large square tower – known as the forebuilding – built against the south side of the White Tower, though this is not documented. Eventually demolished in 1674, this was intended to strengthen the largely unprotected entrance that had previously existed probably for ceremonial not practical purposes.

Much more is known about the development of the castle during the reign of Richard I (1189–99) at the end of the century. When Richard came to the throne he almost immediately departed on a Crusade to the Holy Land, leaving his chancellor, William Longchamp, to administer the realm. Longchamp at once began to improve the defences of the castle, with the constable being allowed the enormous expenditure of £2881 for the forty-nine weeks ending 11 November 1190. The principal task described by the contemporary chronicler, Roger of Howden, was the digging of a deep ditch, which Longchamp hoped to fill with the waters of the Thames. Part of this ditch was uncovered north of the White Tower in 1963–64. It occupied the same north-east to south-west alignment as the earlier Norman ditch, which it almost obliterated, but continued westward in the direction of the Beauchamp Tower, where it presumably turned south to meet the Thames.

Work on the new defences was still in progress when the king's brother, John, entered London on the night of 7/8 October 1191 and rallied an alliance of barons and Londoners to challenge Longchamp's authority. The unpopular bishop fled to the Tower, but was obliged to surrender. One reason for this, as described by the chronicler Matthew Paris in the next century, was the fact that his new moat failed to hold water. Work on the defences must have been completed during the years following Longchamp's banishment.

The work of Longchamp that survives today includes the impressive Bell Tower, on the south-west corner of the Inner Ward, and the adjoining curtain wall to the east. Both rise from a substantial plinth of seven offsets of Sussex marble intended to withstand the action of the Thames. The Bell Tower is unusual in that its shape is octagonal up to the top of the ground floor, thereafter cylindrical. This awkward change might be explained if the tower was built in two stages, the second dating from after the fall of Longchamp.

Cutaway illustration of the Bell Tower showing the upper and lower chambers and the suggested arrangement of the adjoining stair turret and mural passage. (English Heritage)

- AD 1240 -

The Classic Castle

Henry III 1216–72 from a gold penny minted in London

The Tower of London is enlarged to reflect the growing authority of the King, Henry III

The situation the nine-year-old Henry III (1216–72) inherited from his father, King John, in October 1216 could not have been worse. Much of southern England had fallen to the rebellious nobles and their French allies whose leader, Prince Louis, seemed destined to rule the land. However, a number of major strongholds, including Dover and Windsor, stubbornly resisted the French advance allowing Henry's supporters to rally and defeat Prince Louis at the battle of Lincoln in May 1217.

The Tower of London had fallen to King John's enemies at the start of the rebellion in 1215, a fact not lost on Henry III, and doubtless the reason why he spent so much time and effort improving its defences during his long reign. It was, however, the residential complex to the south of the White Tower that attracted the earliest attention. Work effectively began in about 1220 with the construction of two towers, the larger being the Wakefield Tower, the other, apparently ready to be roofed in 1225–26, probably being the Lanthorn Tower (rebuilt 1883–84).

Both towers occupied prominent positions on the corners of the ward, and both were constructed with adjoining chamber blocks. Located either side of the great hall (itself rebuilt in the early 1230s), the arrangement seems to represent an early example of a king's and queen's side in royal planning. The suite including the Wakefield Tower was the grandest and intended for Henry. It incorporated a private water-gate hard against the east side of the tower, affording direct access to the apartments on the first floor. The most imposing chamber would have been in the Wakefield Tower itself and here the King would have retired for rest and private conversation. It is in Henry's reign that we have for the first time a clear idea of how the royal lodgings at the Tower were decorated. In 1238, for example, the Queen, Eleanor of Provence, had the walls of her chamber whitewashed and painted with false ashlar (imitation stone) and flowers.

Contemporary with the construction of the Wakefield Tower was the castle's new water-gate immediately to the west. Quickly enlarged into a strong gate-house, it has been known rather misleadingly since the 17th century as the Bloody Tower. In the late 1230s, and at a time when opposition to royal authority was again mounting, the King embarked on a new round of improvements to the Tower. This involved the construction of a new line of defence to the east and north of the existing outer circuit, thereby doubling the size of the castle. Included in the area of the city enclosed by the new defences was the parish church of St Peter ad Vincula, which Henry retained and considerably embellished. The view on page 23 shows the situation shortly before 23 April 1240 when the new gate at the western entrance collapsed 'as if struck by an earthquake' and at a time when the walls of the White Tower were being whitewashed – an act that was to give the building its long-standing name.

Cutaway illustration of the Wakefield Tower showing the original arrangement of the timber floor that separated the two chambers. (English Heritage)

Apogee of the Medieval Castle

Edward I 1272–1307 from a silver penny minted in London

Edward I's building work makes the Tower one of the strongest fortifications in England

Edward I (1272–1307) was a successful warrior king and England's greatest castle builder. After his return from a crusade in 1274, he set about restoring royal authority that had been seriously undermined in the second half of his father's reign. At the Tower, his work, largely carried out between 1275 and 1285, saw the castle transformed into one of the most formidable fortifications in the realm. The programme involved the remodelling of Henry III's western defences and the creation of a narrow outer ward approached by a complex land entrance to the west and a great water-gate to the south. The scale of the operation is reflected in an expenditure of no less than £21,000, more than double that spent on the castle during Henry III's entire reign.

Work began with the excavation of an enormous moat at least 160ft (50m) wide. Between 1275 and 1281 no less than £4,150 was spent on the wages of diggers and hodmen alone (it has been calculated that a medium-sized castle at this time could have been erected for about £1000!). The City wall, broken by the excavation of the new moat, was strengthened by a stout gate-tower known as the Postern Gate.

The new curtain wall was at first a relatively low structure, allowing fire power to be concentrated on the high walls and towers of the Inner Ward. It was strengthened by a bastion on the north-west corner (Legge's Mount) and three square projections (perhaps intended for catapults) at the north end of the east wall. By 1300, however, both wall and bastion had been substantially raised, while another bastion (Brass Mount) was added to the north-east corner.

The south side of the Outer Ward was an area reclaimed from the Thames. The main water-gate of Henry III's time, the Bloody Tower, thus became an inner gate reached by land. Consequently, a new outer water entrance, St Thomas's Tower, was constructed, but on a much grander scale and with splendid accommodation for Edward himself on the first floor. The water-filled basin beneath the building allowed boats to dock inside the castle after the gates (commonly called Traitors' Gate) had been closed. A staircase in the north-east tower led to the apartment above, the principal rooms being a hall and chamber. A bridge to the Wakefield Tower linked these rooms to the existing royal lodgings.

The new western entrance was a formidable affair comprising an inner and outer gatehouse (Byward and Middle towers) with a massive open barbican beyond (Lion Tower) all connected by stone causeways incorporating drawbridge pits. The entrance was usable by the summer of 1281, thus allowing the remodelling of the inner western defences to proceed. The curtain wall here, together with the gigantic Beauchamp Tower midway along its length, displays an original brick lining, evidence for the notable use of more than 350,000 bricks that were imported from Flanders. This was the first major use of this material in England since the demise of the Roman Empire.

The Middle Tower, the central gatehouse of Edward I's new western entrance completed in 1281. This drawing by T. H. Shepherd in 1849 shows the windows and the coat of arms of George I installed in 1718–19. (Guildhall Library)

- AD 1547 -

The Tudor Power House

Henry VIII 1509–47 from a silver testoon (3rd coinage)

The Tower becomes home to Household departments, government offices and an increasing number of prisoners

Whereas the physical limits of the Tower were largely established during the reign of Edward I, the architectural development of the castle was by no means over. Successive monarchs sought to improve the buildings while the functions and institutions that came to dominate the life of the castle continued to grow. For example, the reign of Edward II (1307–27) saw the formation of the Privy Wardrobe at the Tower, an organisation specialising in arms and munitions. At the same time the safekeeping of important state documents was improved by the setting up of a record office in the White Tower chapel.

The following reign of Edward III (1327–77) witnessed much new building work. Some of this may still be seen, including the postern gate against the east side of the Byward Tower, the handsome vault installed during the remodelling of the Bloody Tower, and the lower part of the Cradle Tower, built on the outer curtain wall between the Well Tower and St Thomas's Tower as a private water-gate for the King.

In Richard II's reign (1377–99) a major project involved the extension of the wharf to assume the form that it retains to this day. The work was directed by no less a figure than the poet Geoffrey Chaucer, the then Clerk of the King's Works. During the Wars of the Roses the Tower saw military action in 1460 and again in 1471, on both occasions being bombarded with cannon. These incidents encouraged Edward VI (1464–83) to extend the castle's defences for the last time, with the construction in 1480 of the brick Bulwark about the western entrance. The enclosure was designed both to carry and to resist artillery and as such was very advanced for the period. Also constructed at this time, or shortly afterwards, was the wedge-shaped gun-tower attached to the Byward Barbican overlooking the wharf. Pierced with openings for cannon and handguns, this building provides an important record of how medieval engineers were beginning to adapt fortifications for artillery warfare.

Henry VII (1485–1505) was not a frequent visitor to the Tower, but it was he who, in the first years of the 16th century, created a second court on the east of the old medieval palace. His son, Henry VIII (1507–47), had the royal lodgings renovated in time for the coronation of Anne Boleyn in May 1533. Thereafter Henry rarely, if ever, stayed at the Tower again and Anne only on the occasion of her own execution.

The most significant building of Henry's later years was the Long House of Ordnance erected against the curtain wall north of the White Tower. This timber-framed building 'wherein all the Kinges majestie's store and provicon of artillerie Ordnance and other Municons' could be kept, was constructed between 1545 and 1547 at a cost of £2,894. Another building from this period, and one that still exists, is the Queen's House of 1540. Occupying the angle of the Inner Ward, behind the Bell Tower, these lodgings were built for Sir Edmund Walsingham, Lieutenant of the Tower.

A view of the Queen's House (to the right) and its surroundings in 1720. (Royal Armouries)

- AD 1700 -

Showplace
of the Nation

The Tower increasingly becomes a military store and workshop, and a national museum of military might

View of the interior of a model of the Grand Storehouse showing the east end of the Small Armoury of 1696. Against the end wall may be seen the figure of a great organ its pipes were made out of brass blunderbusses and two thousand pairs of pistols. This is flanked by a 'fiery serpent' and a 'seven-headed Monster' made of pistols and wooden carvings. (Royal Armouries)

Later Tudor monarchs made only symbolic use of the Tower as a residence, usually on the eve of the coronation procession to Westminster Abbey. In March 1604 James I performed the traditional lodging for the last time. The palace buildings were by now quite dilapidated, as demonstrated by the great hall whose roof and walls were covered with giant pieces of canvas to keep out the weather.

In 1639 permission was given to the Ordnance Office to convert the hall into a military store and three years later the Master of the Ordnance occupied the old King's Lodgings in and around the Lanthorn Tower. By then other buildings formerly associated with court life had been turned into military stores, including most of the White Tower.

This process continued during the Commonwealth and accelerated after the restoration of the monarchy in 1660, when the Tower stores were found to be inadequate to receive the arms being recovered from around the country. Consequently, in January 1663, a new storehouse was ordered to be built in the old palace garden to the south-east of the White Tower. The result, the present New Armouries building, was finished by 8 November 1664.

Two years later an ambitious programme to convert the old medieval palace to the south of the White Tower into a complex of Ordnance store, offices and lodgings began. A plan to improve the powder magazine in the White Tower was abandoned, however, after the disastrous Dutch raid on the Medway in June 1667.

In 1679–80, to counter the continuing Dutch threat, the riverside defences were improved and between 1682 and 1686, against a backdrop of internal dissent, a more extensive plan to modernise the landward defences was implemented. The western entrance was reformed, numerous gun platforms were installed along the inner and outer defences, and new accommodation for an enlarged garrison provided. Despite these measures the Tower fell into the hands of James II's enemies, without a shot being fired, in 1688.

By the end of the 17th century the role of the Tower as the central arsenal of the nation was drawing to a close as other depots in southern England, such as Plymouth, Portsmouth, Chatham and Woolwich, were being developed. This is reflected in the increasing use of parts of the Tower for public displays. For example the Grand Storehouse, erected against the north curtain wall facing the White Tower in 1688–92, appears to have had its design altered to receive a remarkable display known as the Small Armoury. Occupying the entire first floor, the armoury comprised tens of thousands of small arms, and a mass of specially commissioned carvings, arranged into such diverse figures as pyramids, the 'Back Bones of a Whale', the 'Waves of the Sea' and a pair of ceremonial gates. Perhaps not surprisingly the 18th-century historian William Maitland described it as a sight 'no one ever beheld without Astonishment ... not to be matched perhaps in the world'.

Engraved view of the Tower of London from the river by Wenceslaus Hollar published in 1647. (Royal Armouries)

- AD 1841 -

The Great Conflagration

Victoria 1837–1901 from a gold pattern £5 piece, 1839

Life at the Tower is disrupted by three fires, the loss of the Mint, and the end of the Menagerie

The life of the Tower changed little throughout the 18th century as the official departments and the inhabitants carried on with their duties and daily routines. At the start of George I's reign (1714–27) the state of the defences was again reviewed and the batteries re-organised to improve their effectiveness. That said, the fortifications were hopelessly out of date and a visiting Portuguese merchant was probably correct when he observed that the place 'would not hold out four and twenty hours against an army prepared for a siege'.

The Ordnance regularly repaired and/or replaced the lodgings assigned to its officers and officials. Some of this work can still be seen in the terrace of four houses (Old Hospital Block) for clerks built in 1718–19 on the east side of the White Tower and another clerk's house (No. 2 Tower Green) constructed in 1736 next to the Chaplain's residence. The Middle Tower, which formed the residence of the Ordnance Barrack Master, also exhibits evidence of its refurbishment in 1718–19, including the coat of arms of George I over the gate passage. The accommodation of the

garrison also received regular attention, and in 1752 the principal barracks in the Outer Ward, between the Salt and Broad Arrow towers, were reconstructed.

The largest single building operation undertaken at the Tower during the 18th century was the reconstruction of the Ordnance administrative office south of the White Tower following a spectacular fire in 1774. The clearance that preceded construction saw much of what remained of the medieval and Tudor palace disappear, including the Lanthorn Tower. Ready for occupation in the autumn of 1780, the new building was seriously damaged by a second fire in 1788, and during its renovation the former medieval great hall to the west was demolished to make way for an office extension and a new storehouse.

The outbreak of the Napoleonic Wars in 1803 and the great increase in demand for arms saw the setting up of an 'Arms Manufactory' at the east end of the wharf. This closed in 1815, but the buildings remained for another 50 years. In 1812 the Royal Mint abandoned its workshops in the Outer Ward for new premises to the north-west of the Tower, thus ending more than 500 years of coin production in the castle. In 1835, after more than 600 years, the Royal Menagerie finally closed, though like the Mint its buildings in and about the Lion Tower survived for the time being.

The tourist attractions were enhanced with the construction of a new museum for the Tower Armouries against the south side of the White Tower in 1825 and a new Jewel House against the Martin Tower in 1840–41. In 1838 the price of viewing the Armouries was cut from 3 shillings to 1 shilling and in the following year it was lowered again to 6d. The effect was to see visitor numbers rise from 10,500 to 80,000 per annum. These improvements, however, were overshadowed by a terrible fire that destroyed the Grand Storehouse and most of its contents on the evening of 31 October 1841 – the greatest single disaster to have beset the Tower.

A view of the Tower by Thomas Shotter Boys shortly before the fire of 30 October 1841 destroyed the Grand Storehouse. (Royal Armouries)

- AD 1890 -

Remedievalisation of the Castle

Victoria 1837–1901 from a gold Diamond Jubilee medal, 1897

The Tower becomes a mass tourist attraction and its image as a medieval castle is revived

etween the spring of 1843 and the end of 1845 life at the Tower was greatly disrupted by an operation to drain and partially infill the filthy and polluted moat. Even before this was finished, construction of a great new barrack block on the site of the Grand Storehouse had begun. Amid much ceremony on 15 June 1845, the Duke of Wellington, Constable of the Tower, laid the foundation stone of the building, the Waterloo Barracks, named in celebration of his greatest victory. The barracks were built to house nearly 1,000 soldiers and cost over £30,000. The architectural style, described as 'castellated Gothic of the fifteenth century', was clearly intended to harmonise with the medieval aspects of the castle and was devised by the Royal Engineers under the command of Major Lewis Alexander Hall. So too was the new officers' lodgings and mess (now the headquarters and museum of the Royal Regiment of Fusiliers) and the reconstructed towers behind the barracks.

The barracks and their surroundings were finished by 1850, just ahead of the arrival of Anthony Salvin, the eminent

Victorian architect most associated with the restoration of the Tower. Salvin was first consulted about the Beauchamp Tower in 1851 after the Office of Works considered a proposal to open the building to the public. In the following year various accretions were removed and thereafter the external walls of the tower were refaced, windows and doorways replaced and battlements recreated.

In the wake of the subsequent withdrawal of the Record Office and the gradual phasing out of War Office stores, workshops and offices, this pattern of restoration was to be rehearsed on many other buildings. By 1870 Salvin had completed major repairs and alterations to the Salt Tower, White Tower, St Thomas's Tower and Wakefield Tower (in that order). In addition he provided the external design for the Casemates in the Outer Ward and had designed and supervised the building of the Pump House (now the Tower Shop) at the western entrance and the pair of Tudor-style houses immediately west of the Bloody Tower.

After Salvin, John Taylor, the Office of Works architect who was subsequently knighted for his endeavours, directed restorations. Taylor exercised a very thorough approach to restoration or 're-creation' as much of it might more accurately be described. Under his supervision many historically important buildings were demolished or needlessly altered, simply because they did no comply with an aesthetic idea of what a medieval castle should look like. Some of the worse excesses were associated with the clearance of the Inmost Ward and the 'reconstruction' of the curtain defences between the Wakefield and Salt towers in 1879–88. However, this was the last phase of the 'remedievalisation' process. For as Thackeray Turner, Secretary of the Society for the Protection of Ancient Buildings, wrote in 1883 'the notion of building a medieval Tower to show what England was like in the 13th century will finally be given up and in place of it a respect for genuine remains of former times will prevail'. This prediction was about to be fulfilled.

ABOVE *A photograph of St Thomas's Tower taken shortly before June 1862 when part of the south-east turret collapsed. Note the tarpaulin in front of Traitors' Gate, intended to provide privacy for the soldiers of the garrison who used the water-filled basin below the building as a sort of large bathing pool! (G. Parnell)*

BELOW *The same view of St Thomas's Tower after the restoration of the building in 1864–66. (G. Parnell)*

- AD 1940 -

The Castle at War

George VI 1936–52 from a 3d piece, 1937

The two World Wars see a revival of the Tower as a state prison and place of execution

The last building of the 19th century was the Main Guard, a four-storey, Jacobean-styled, structure erected north of the Wakefield Tower. Constructed in brick with stone dressings between December 1898 and July 1900 it contained, in addition to the guardroom, an orderly room, office, stores, recreation area, mess and lecture rooms.

After the hectic round of Victorian restorations, works in the Tower during the early 20th century appeared restrained. Old habits die hard, however, and in the years either side of the Great War (1914–18) some rather heavy-handed works were undertaken. These included the conversion of Brass Mount into a military store in 1908, the removal of the impressive clock faces from the north-east turret of the White Tower and alterations to the Queen's House in 1913, and the removal of interesting accretions from the Byward Tower and the destructive refurbishment of the old Warders' Hall (now the Water Lane Shop) in the 1920s.

The greatest impact on the life and fabric of the Tower in the 20th century, however, was brought about by the two World Wars.

During the Great War, the air raid – a new and terrifying feature of warfare – sometimes disrupted visits to the castle. At the start of hostilities the Kaiser had specifically instructed his military commanders not to target the royal palaces and historic monuments of London, but as the war dragged on the threat to the Tower increased. During one of the heaviest raids on 13 June 1917, a bomb landed in the moat near Legge's Mount. It failed to explode and the only reported casualties were two pigeons.

During the Great War the Tower staged a revival as a state prison and place of execution. Eleven German spies were shot within the precincts between November 1914 and April 1916. During the Second World War (1939–45) some 180 men passed through the castle on their way to prison camps in the north of England. Most were U-boat men and Luftwaffe airmen. There were, however, two notable prisoners – Herr Gerlach, the German Consul General to Iceland, and Rudulf Hess, the Deputy Führer of Germany. The role of the Tower as a state prison finally ended on 14 August 1941 when the convicted German spy Josef Jacobs was executed by firing squad.

Aerial bombardment during the Second World War caused considerable damage, notably between September and December 1940 when attacks on London were at their most intense. One of the heaviest raids – as depicted here – was on the night of 29 December. Sirens heralding the approach of the German aircraft were sounded at 6.10pm and the 'all clear' at 11.40pm. During this time thousands of incendiary bombs and other devices were dropped on the City. The destruction around the Tower was considerable, an army officer reported that the flames 'created an awesome spectacle and one that those who saw it will never forget'. At about 7.30pm two or three incendiaries landed on the roof of the Main Guard and a fire soon took hold. A valiant effort was made to save the building, but strong winds and a lack of water pressure sealed its fate.

The North Bastion, built midway along the outer northern curtain wall in 1856, after being wrecked by a high-explosive bomb on 5 October 1940. Sadly the occupant, Yeoman Warder Reeves, lost his life during the incident. (Royal Armouries)

- AD 2000 -

The Tower
Today

Elizabeth II 1952–present, portrait coinage head by Ian Rank Broadley introduced in 1998

Archaeologists excavating part of the Lion Tower, the site of the Royal Menagerie, in April 1999. (Richard Bradley)

Archaeological and documentary research reveals new evidence of the Tower's history

At the outbreak of hostilities in 1939 public admission to the Tower was suspended while the Crown Jewels and important parts of the Armouries were evacuated, the former to a location that has never been disclosed. Privilege tours for Dominion and Allied troops were organised, but it was not until 1 January 1946, several months after the agony of war had ended, that the castle reopened its gates to the public. By then much of the damage had been made good and the exhibits reinstated. The Tower quickly re-established itself as one of the nation's most popular attractions and now annually attracts over 2½ million visitors.

The steady growth in tourism has, to some extent, been achieved at the expense of what remained of the institutional life of the castle. The garrison has dwindled to a small contingent retained for guard and ceremonial duties, while the role of the Tower as a military supply base, its oldest function, ended virtually unnoticed in 1994 with the withdrawal of the Royal

Logistic Corps. In 1984 the last of the skilled craftsmen closed their workshops and departed. Twelve years later most of the staff of the Armouries (renamed Royal Armouries in 1985) and much of its collection, left for a purpose-built museum in Leeds in Yorkshire.

That said, the Tower remains a living institution managed by a Resident Governor and his staff and with a ceremonial life that continues unabated. More than one hundred people still inhabit the castle's confines and more than two hundred work there during the day. It remains, too, the headquarters of the Royal Regiment of Fusiliers, raised here in 1685, while the Royal Armouries, the descendant of the medieval armoury, continues to display an important part of its collection in the White Tower as well as maintaining a library and education centre. Some of the recent changes to the castle have provided opportunities to investigate its past, to open new areas to public view and to improve the way it displays its treasures and caters for visitor needs. In this process, visitors' understanding of the unique and fascinating story of the Tower of London and its site has been enhanced.

The Line of Kings, one of the Tower's historic displays dating from 1660. The story of this remarkable exhibition is now told in one of the Royal Armouries' galleries in the White Tower, redisplayed between 1996 and 1998. (Royal Armouries)

Tower Plan

- *Buildings open to the public are numbered in red*

1	Beauchamp Tower	
2	Bell Tower	
3	Bloody Tower	
4	Bowyer Tower	
5	Brass Mount	
6	Brick Tower	
7	Broad Arrow Tower	
8	Byward Tower	
9	Casemates	
10	Chapel Royal of St Peter ad Vincula	
11	Coldharbour Gate (remains)	
12	Constable Tower	
13	Cradle Tower	
14	Devereux Tower	
15	Develin Tower	
16	Flint Tower	
17	Fusiliers' Museum	
18	Hospital Block	
19	Henry III's Watergate	
20	Lanthorn Tower	
21	Legge's Mount	
22	Line of the Roman City Wall	
23	Lion Tower Drawbridge Pit	
24	Martin Tower	
25	Middle Tower	
26	Mint Street	
27	New Armouries	
28	Queen's House	
29	Salt Tower	
30	Scaffold Site	
31	Site of the Great Hall	
32	St Thomas's Tower	
33	Tower Green	
34	Tower Hill Memorial	
35	Traitors' Gate	
36	Wakefield Tower	
37	Wall of the Inmost Ward	
38	Wardrobe Tower	
39	Water Lane	
40	Waterloo Barracks, Crown Jewels	
41	Well Tower	
42	Wharf	
43	White Tower	

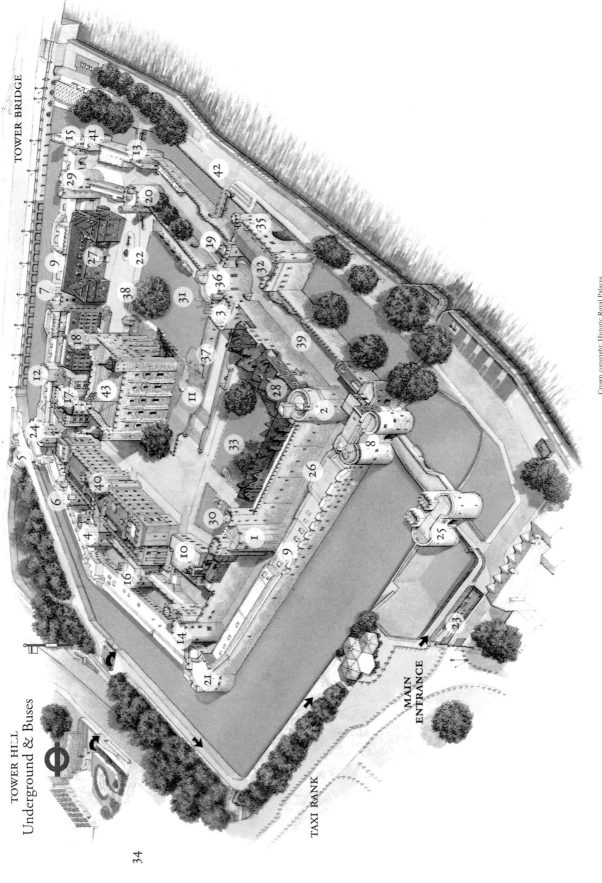

TOWER BRIDGE

TOWER HILL
Underground & Buses

15
41
13
42
29
20
19
35
9
7
27
22
32
38
36
31
3
18
37
11
12
39
17
43
28
24
2
33
8
5
26
40
6
25
4
30
16
1
10
9
14
23
21
34

MAIN
ENTRANCE

TAXI RANK

First published in Great Britain in 2000 by Osprey Publishing
Elms Court, Chapel Way, Botley, Oxford OX2 9LP, UK
E-mail: info@ospreypublishing.com

CIP Data for this publication is available from the British Library

ISBN 1 84176 170 2

Editor: Jane Penrose
Designer: Rebecca Smart

Origination by Valhaven Ltd, Isleworth, UK
Printed through Bookbuilders, Hong Kong

04 05 06   10 9 8 7 6 5 4

FOR A CATALOGUE OF ALL BOOKS PUBLISHED BY
OSPREY MILITARY AND AVIATION, PLEASE CONTACT:

The Marketing Manager, Osprey Direct UK, PO Box 140,
Wellingborough, Northants, NN8 2FA, United Kingdom
E-mail: info@ospreydirect.co.uk

The Marketing Manager, Osprey Direct USA,
c/o MBI Publishing, PO Box 1, 729 Prospect Ave,
Osceola, WI54020, USA
E-mail: info@ospreydirectusa.com

COIN CREDITS
pp4, 13 courtesy of the Museum of London
pp7, 10, 16, 19, 22, 25, 28, 31, 34, 37, 40 courtesy of the Trustees
  of the British Museum
p43 courtesy of the Royal Mint

**Back cover image courtesy of the Board of the Trustees of
the Armouries**